MEGAHITS of 2013

23 Pop, Rock, Country, TV, and Movie Chartbusters

Contents

Alfred Music
P.O. Box 10003
Van Nuys, CA 91410-0003
alfred.com

Printed in USA.

ISBN-10: 1-4706-1022-1
ISBN-13: 978-1-4706-1022-7

BLOWN AWAY

Words and Music by
JOSH KEAR
and CHRIS TOMPKINS

4

Chorus:

Shat-ter ev-ery win-dow 'til it's all blown a - way._____ Ev - ery

brick, ev-ery board, ev-ery slam-ming door, blown a - way_____ 'til there's

noth-ing left stand - ing, noth-ing left of yes - ter-day._____ Ev - ery

tear - soaked whis - key mem-o-ry blown a - way,_____ blown_____ a - way,

Verse 2:

6

Some peo-ple call it tak - ing shel - ter; she called it sweet re - venge.

Chorus:

Shat-ter ev - ery win - dow 'til it's all blown a - way. Ev - ery

brick, ev - ery board, ev - ery slam-ming door, blown a - way 'til there's

noth-ing left stand - ing, noth-ing left of yes - ter-day. Ev - ery

8

ANYTHING COULD HAPPEN

Words and Music by
ELLIE GOULDING and JAMES ELIOT

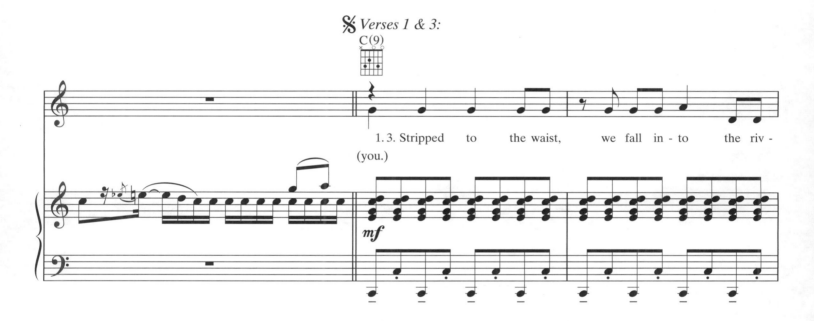

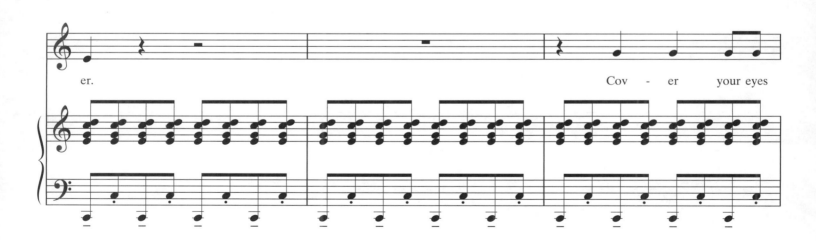

Verse 2:

2. Af - ter the war we said we'd fight to - geth - er.

I guess we thought that's just what hu - mans do,___

___ let - ting dark - ness grow, as if we need it's pal -

14

ette and we need its col - our. But now I've seen it

Dm11 Fmaj9

through, and now I know the truth that an - y - thing could hap - pen, an - y - thing could

Dm11

hap - pen, an - y - thing could hap - pen, an - y - thing could hap - pen, an - y - thing could

Fmaj9 C

hap - pen, an - y - thing could hap - pen, an - y - thing could...

cresc.

f

Bridge:

Ba - by, I'll give you ev - 'ry - thing you

need._____ I'll give you ev - 'ry - thing you need,_ ah._____

CATCH MY BREATH

Words and Music by
JASON HALBERT, KELLY CLARKSON
and ERIC OLSON

Moderately fast pop rock ♩ = 126

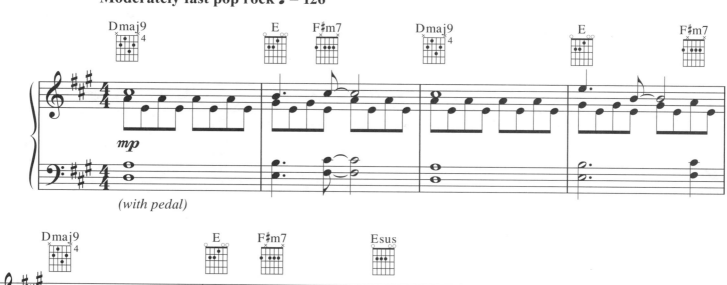

(with pedal)

1. I don't wan-na be left

Verse 1 (Sing 1st time only):

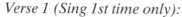

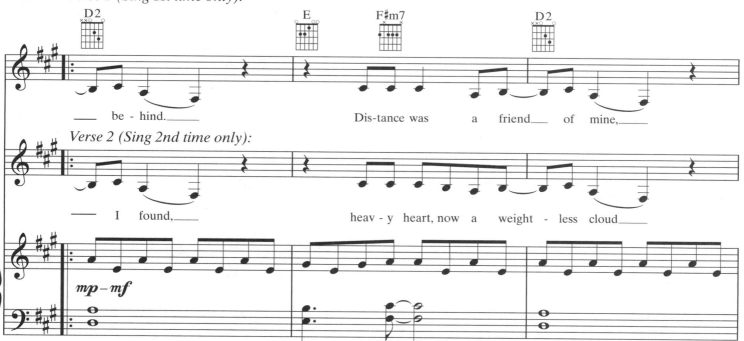

— be - hind.___ Dis-tance was a friend___ of mine,___

Verse 2 (Sing 2nd time only):

— I found,___ heav-y heart, now a weight-less cloud___

Catch My Breath - 7 - 1

Chorus:

DOWNTON ABBEY - THE SUITE

Composed by
JOHN LUNN

Allegro con spirito ♩ = 165

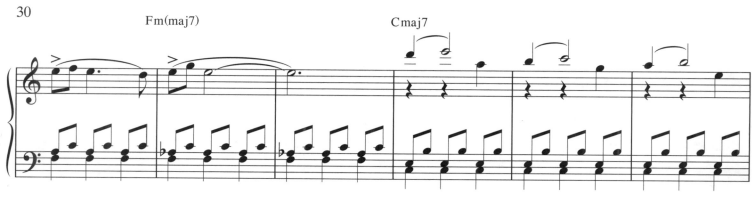

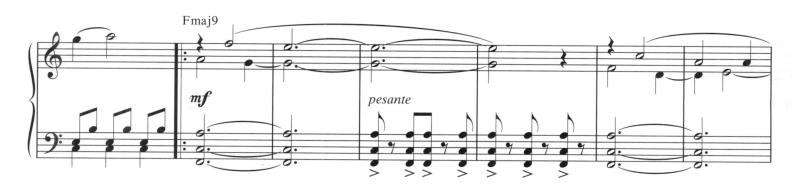

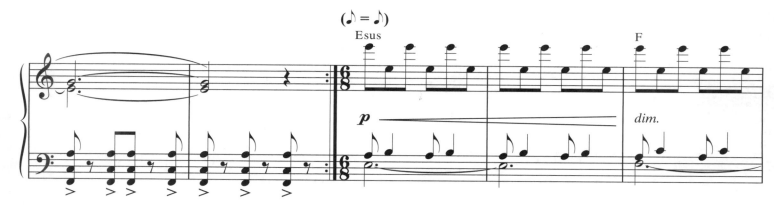

Poco meno mosso ♩ = 154

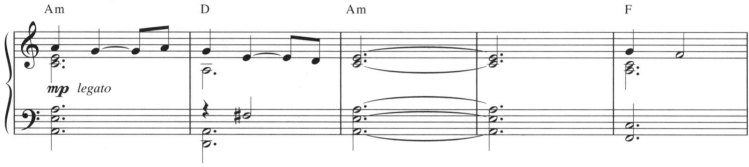

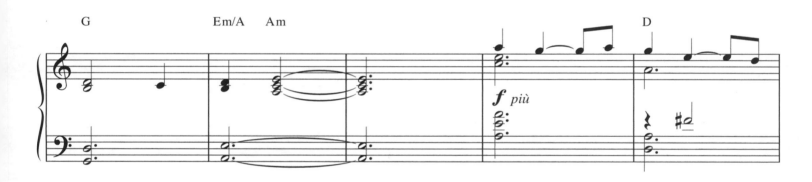

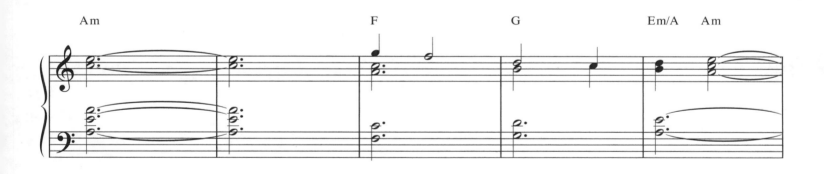

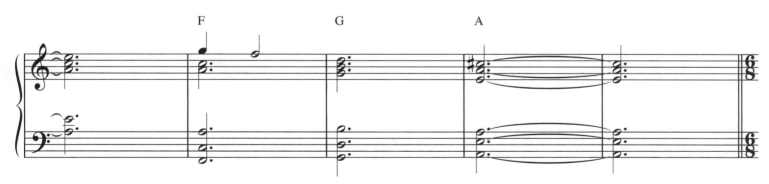

Tempo I (♩. = 112)

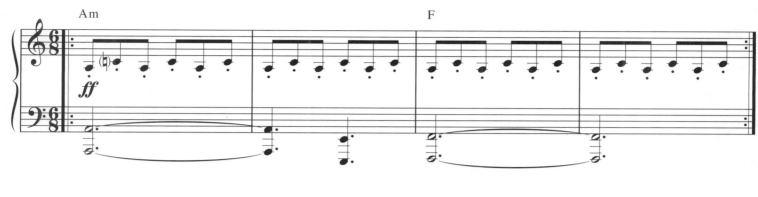

EVERYBODY TALKS

Words and Music by
TYLER GLENN and TIM PAGNOTTA

Moderately fast rock ♩ = 152

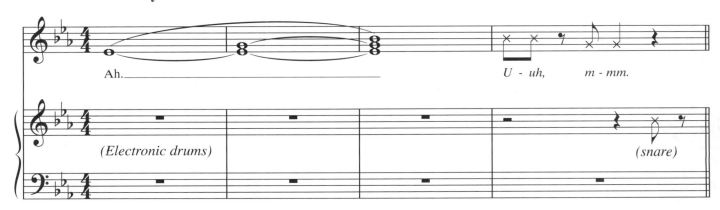

Ah.___ U - uh, m - mm.

(Electronic drums) (snare)

Verse 1:

1. Hey, ba - by, won't you look my way,___ I can be your new___ ad - dic-

mf

tion.___ Hey ba - by, what you got - ta say?___ All you're

42

Verse 2:

2. Hey, hon-ey, you could be my drug.__ You could be my new__ pre-scrip-

tion.__ Too much could be an o-ver-dose.__ All this

trash talk make__ me itch-in'._____ Oh, my, my, s***,

ev-'ry-bod-y talks, ev-'ry-bod-y talks, ev-'ry-bod-y talks *too much.* It start-ed with a

GIRL ON FIRE

Words and Music by
BILLY SQUIER, JEFFREY BHAKSER,
ALICIA KEYS and SALAAM REMI

Moderately, with a heavy beat ♩ = 92

Verse 1: (Sing first time only)

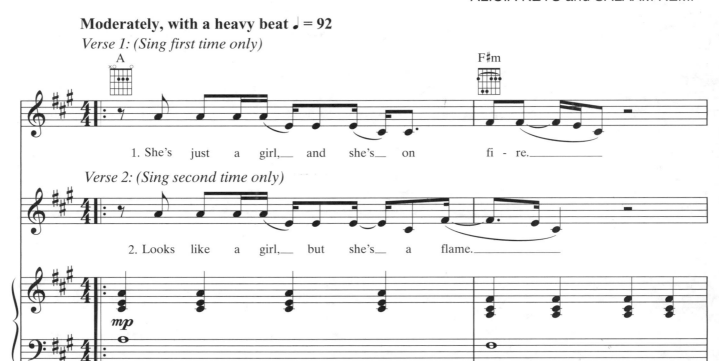

1. She's just a girl, and she's on fi - re.

Verse 2: (Sing second time only)

2. Looks like a girl, but she's a flame.

Hot - ter than a fan - ta - sy, lone - ly like a high - way.

So bright, she can burn your eyes, bet - ter look the oth - er way.

Girl on Fire - 7 - 1

51

Girl on Fire - 7 - 4

Chorus:

GIVE YOUR HEART A BREAK

Words and Music by
BILL STEINBERG
and JOSH ALEXANDER

Moderate dance rock ($\\text{♩} = 124$)

*Original recording in G♭.

Give Your Heart a Break - 7 - 1

Chorus:

There's just so much you can take.__ Give your heart a break.__ Let me give your heart a break,

__ your heart a break,__ oh, yeah, yeah. The day__ I

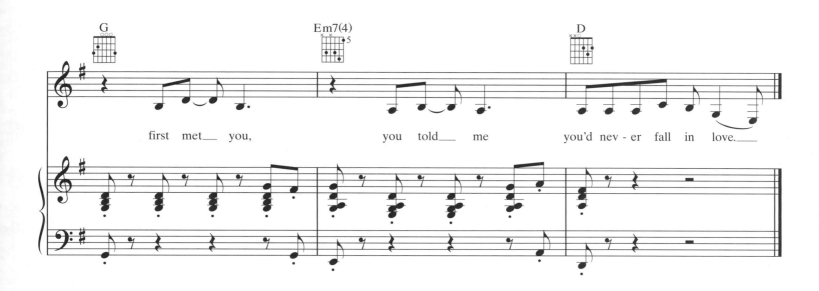

first met__ you, you told__ me you'd nev-er fall in love.__

GOOD MORNING BEAUTIFUL

Words and Music by
JIM BRICKMAN and LUKE McMASTER

Verse 1:

1. I hear the a-larm go off at six, used to be I'd wan-na call in sick.

Good Morning Beautiful - 10 - 1

E B C♯m A
I al-ways dread - ed this time of day, but not an - y - more 'cause of you,
E B N.C.
smil - in' you, per - fect you. Good morn - ing,
Chorus:
E B C♯m A E B
beau - ti - ful. I know it's gon - na be a good morn - ing, beau - ti - ful. When you're
C♯m F♯ A B
wak - ing up with me it's gon - na be a good morn - ing, beau - ti - ful.

Bridge:

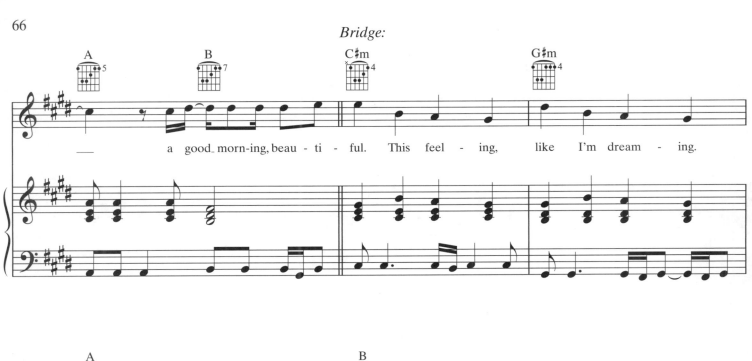

a good morn-ing, beau - ti - ful. This feel - ing, like I'm dream - ing.

It's a dream come true, when I wake_ up with you._

_ La la la la la la la la._

La la la la la la la, la la la la la la.

Verse 3:

68

GOOD TIME

Words and Music by
MATTHEW THIESSEN,
BRIAN LEE and ADAM YOUNG

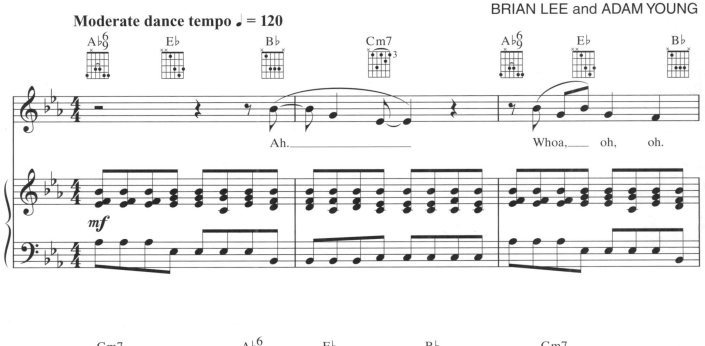

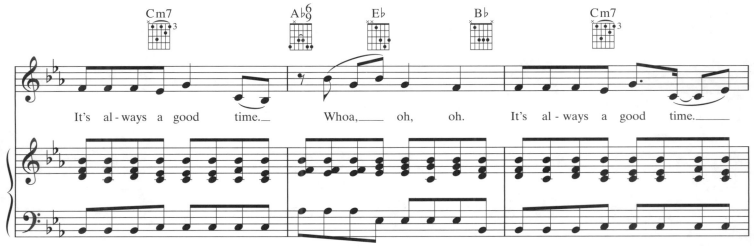

Good Time - 6 - 1

right side of the bed. What's up with this Prince song in-side my head?

Hands up if you're down to get down to-night,_____ 'cuz

Verses 2 & 3:

it's al-ways a good time.___

2. Slept in all my clothes like I did-n't care.
3. Freaked out, dropped my phone in the pool a-gain.

Hopped in - to a cab, take me an - y-where.
Checked out of my room, hit the A. T. M.

I'm in if you're
Let's hang out if you're

HARD TO LOVE

Words and Music by
BILLY MONTANA,
JOHN OZIER and BEN GLOVER

Hard to Love - 7 - 1

Verse:

Chorus:

You love me good._____

HOME

Words and Music by
DREW PEARSON and GREG HOLDEN

Moderately ♩ = 120

Verse 1:

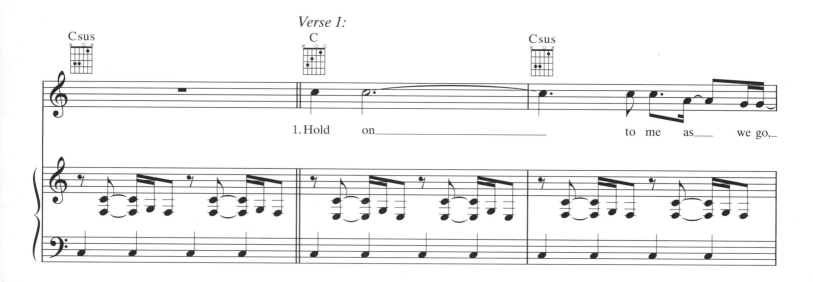

1. Hold on to me as we go,

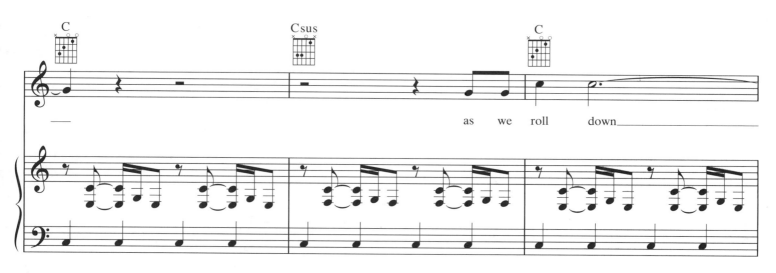

as we roll down

Home - 5 - 1

Home - 5 - 3

LIGHTS

Words and Music by
ELLIE GOULDING, RICHARD STANNARD
and ASHLEY HOWES

Lights - 6 - 1

I need to push me. You show the
ly time I feel safe. You show the

‰ *Chorus:*

lights that stop me turn to stone, you shine me when I'm a - lone.

And so I tell my - self that I'll be strong and

MISTY MOUNTAINS

(from *The Hobbit: An Unexpected Journey*)

Lyrics Adapted by
FRAN WALSH and PHILIPPA BOYENS

Music by
DAVID DONALDSON, DAVID LONG,
STEVE ROCHE and JANET RODDICK

Moderate chant, sung freely (♩ = 104)

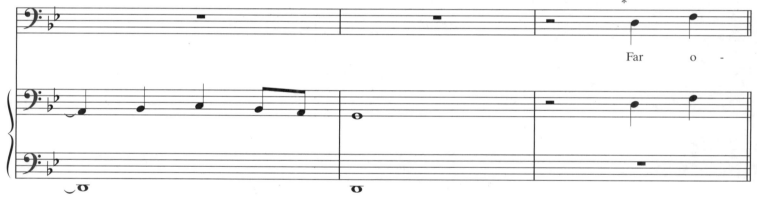

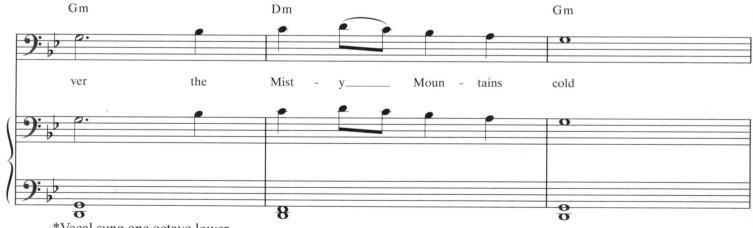

*Vocal sung one octave lower.

Misty Mountains - 3 - 1

PEOPLE LIKE US

Words and Music by
BLAIR DALY, MEGHAN KABIR
and JAMES MICHAEL

Pre-Chorus:

times.___ Oh,___ peo - ple like us, we've got - ta stick to-geth - er. Keep your head up, noth-ing lasts for - ev - er. Here's to the damned, to the lost and for-got - ten. It's hard to get high when you're liv - ing on the bot - tom.___ Oh,___ woah,_____ oh,___ woah._____ We are all

Chorus:

N.C.

f

SILVER LINING
(Crazy 'Bout You)

Words and Music by
DIANE WARREN

*Original recording in F♯ major.

THINKIN BOUT YOU

Words and Music by
SHEA TAYLOR
and CHRISTOPHER BREAUX

Slowly ♩ = 63

N.C.

mp

A tor-

Verse 1: (Sing first time only)

Fmaj7　Dm7　Em7　Am

na - do flew a - round　my room_ be-fore you came. Ex-cuse_ the mess it made, it us - 'lly does-n't rain_ in

Verse 2: (Sing second time only)

like you, I just thought you were cool_ e-nough to kick it. Got a　beach house I could sell you in I - da-ho. Since you think I don't

Fmaj7　Em7　E♭maj7　Dm7

South-ern Cal-i-for - nian, much_like A - ri - zo - na. My　eyes don't　shed　tears_ but boy, they bawl_ when I'm

love you, I just thought you were cute,_ that's why I kissed you. Got-ta fight-er jet, I don't get to fly_ it, though. I'm ly-in' down

Thinkin Bout You - 4 - 1

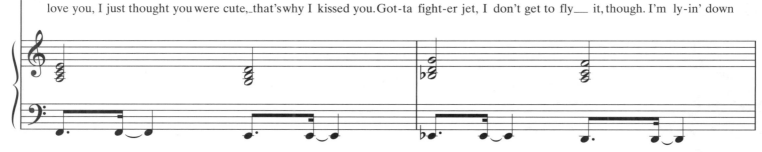

116

TWO HEARTS BREAKING

Words and Music by
JEWEL MURRAY

Chorus:

Bridge:

break - ing.__ I'm__ dry heav - ing tears from cry - ing all__

__ these years. And I know__ this is__ your night - mare come true.__ I

Verse:

nev - er want - ed this__ for you,_ but... I'm__ the teeth, you're the heart._ To - geth-

er we're the start__ of the in - hale and the scream._ You're the not_

SEE YOU AGAIN

Words and Music by
CARRIE UNDERWOOD,
DAVID HODGES and HILLARY LINDSEY

Gtr. tuned down 1/2 step:

⑥ = E♭   ③ = G♭
⑤ = A♭   ② = B♭
④ = D♭   ① = E♭

Moderate rock ♩ = 100

Oh,_____ oh,_____ oh,_____

oh,_____ oh,_____ oh,_____

See You Again - 8 - 1

Verse 1 (sing 1st time only):

1. Said good-bye, turned a - round, and you were gone,___ gone,___ gone,___

Verse 2 (sing 2nd time only):

2. I can hear those ech - oes in the wind___ at___ night___

fad - ed in - to the set - ting___ sun,___ slipped a - way.___

call - ing me back___ in___ time,___ back to you___

Bridge:

Some - times___ I feel my___ heart___ is___ break - ing. But

I stay strong___ and I hold___ on___ 'cuz I know...___

A VERY RESPECTABLE HOBBIT

(from *The Hobbit: An Unexpected Journey*)

Music by
HOWARD SHORE

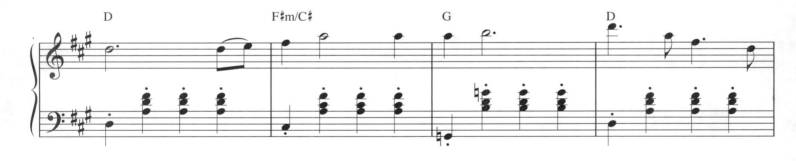

A Very Respectable Hobbit - 2 - 1

SUIT & TIE

Words and Music by
SHAWN CARTER, JEROME HARMON, TERRANCE STUBBS,
JOHNNY WILSON, CHARLES STILL, TIM MOSLEY,
JUSTIN TIMBERLAKE and JAMES FAUNTLEROY

Suit & Tie - 11 - 1

With a dance groove

Verse 1: (Sing 1st time only)

wait 'til I get you on the floor,_ good look-in'.   Babe,

Verse 2: (Sing 2nd time only)

let me get a good look at it.   Ooh,_ so

_ go-in' out so hot,   just_ like an ov-en.   And I'll_____

thick,   now I know why they call_ it a fat-ty.   And aw,_

_ burn_ my-self, but just_ had to touch it.   But it's_ so

s*** so sick, got a hit and picked_ up a hab-it.   That's_ al-

noth - in' but a lit- tle doo - zy when_ she does it. She's_ so

kill- er, my thrill-er, yeah,_ you're a class-ic. And you're_ all

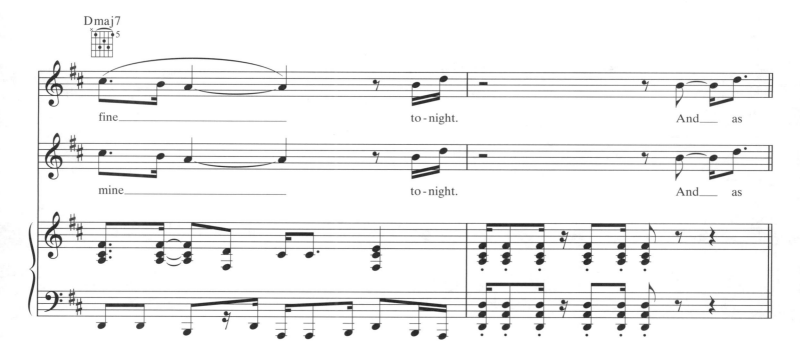

Dmaj7

fine_____ to - night. And_ as

mine_____ to - night. And_ as

Chorus:

Em9

long as I got my suit and tie,___ I'm - a leave it all on the floor to - night.___

Rap:

All black at the white shows. White shoes at the black shows. Green card for the Cuban linx.
Y'all sit back and enjoy the light show. Nothin' exceeds like excess. Stoute got gout from havin' the best of the best.
Is this what it's all about? I'm at the restaurant, my rant disturbin' the guests, years of distress, tears on the dress.
Tryin' to hide her face with some make-up sex. Uhh, this is truffle season. Tom Ford tuxedoes for no reason.
All saints for my angel. Alexander Wang, too. Ass-tight denim and some Dunks, I'll show you how to do this young!
Uhh, no papers, catch vapors. Get high, out Vegas. D'usses on doubles, ain't lookin' for trouble.
You just got good genes so a n**** try'n cuff you. Tell your mother that I love her 'cause I love you.
Tell your father we go farther as a couple. They ain't lose a daughter, got a son. I show you how to do this, hon'.

WAGON WHEEL

Words and Music by
KETCH SECOR
and BOB DYLAN

Verse 1 (Sing 1st time only):

1. Head-in' down south to the land of the pines. I'm thumb-in' my way out of North

Verse 2 (Sing 2nd time only):

2. Run - in' from the cold up in New Eng - land, I was born to be a fid - dler in an old-

Wagon Wheel - 9 - 1

Rock___ me, ma-ma, like the wind and the rain.___ Rock___

me, ma-ma, like a south-bound train. Hey,___

To Coda ⊕

ma-ma, rock___ me.

1.

dim.

2.

(Inst. solo ad lib....

Wagon Wheel - 9 - 9

WHAT ARE YOU GOING TO DO WHEN YOU ARE NOT SAVING THE WORLD

(from *Man of Steel*)

Composed by
HANS ZIMMER

WHEN I WAS YOUR MAN

Words and Music by
PHILIP LAWRENCE, ANDREW WYATT,
BRUNO MARS and ARI LEVINE

Verse 1: (Sing first time only)

1. Same bed but it feels just a lit-tle bit big - ger now,

Verse 2: (Sing second time only)

2. My pride, my e-go, my needs and my self - ish ways

our song on the ra-di-o, but it don't sound___ the same.

'caused a good strong wom-an like you to walk out___ my life.

Now I'll

When I Was You Man - 6 - 1